GREECE

© Aladdin Books Ltd 1987

Designed and produced by
Aladdin Books Ltd
70 Old Compton Street
London W1

*First published in the
United States in 1987 by*
Franklin Watts
387 Park Avenue South
New York, NY 10016

ISBN 0 531 10398 6

Library of Congress Catalog
Card Number: 87-50224

Design   David West
               Children's Book Design

Editor   Denny Robson

Researcher   Cecilia Weston-Baker

Illustrator   Rob Shone

Consultant   Patsy Vanags,
               Education Office,
               British Museum, London.

Printed in Belgium

CONTENTS

GREAT CIVILIZATIONS

GREECE

1600–30 BC

Anton Powell

FRANKLIN WATTS
New York · London · Toronto · Sydney

INTRODUCTION

The ancient Greeks were among the liveliest and most creative people ever to have lived. Their towns and villages were the scene of colorful festivals, noisy parties – and savage warfare. Storytellers told tales of love, war and adventure, sometimes passing on with wonderful accuracy details from prehistoric times. Critical thinkers developed ideas about religion and the human mind which are still found useful today.

The Greeks learned to use a form of writing which is the ancestor of our alphabet. Drama was a Greek invention. So was the idea of democracy, organized politics which allowed ordinary men to control their own towns.

Ancient Greece was made up of hundreds of independent towns. Greeks probably could have conquered huge areas of Europe and Asia, but these little towns loved their independence and they never united to form an unbeatable force.

Eventually a ruler from the fringe of the Greek world, Alexander, came to control Greece. Adapting Greek methods of fighting, he quickly conquered almost the whole of the Middle East spreading Greek language and customs.

This book looks at Greek civilization from about 1600 BC to the last century BC. There are four main periods: the age of the Mycenaeans; the era of expansion; the golden age of Athens; and the Hellenistic period.

The Greeks made progress as thinkers partly because they could criticize and laugh at themselves. Here is the festival of Dionysus, god of wine. Part of the festival, at Athens, was comic drama in which even the great were teased. For example, the wise politician Pericles was known to keep Athens safe from its grim enemy, Sparta. Pericles was much admired, but at the festival people called him "onion-head" and said he was as pompous as the god Zeus!

THE MYCENAEANS c1600-1150 BC

The first great civilization of the Greek mainland is named after the town of Mycenae. We know of this civilization from archaeological excavations, and from the poetry of the Greeks themselves. The language of the Mycenaeans was Greek. Their style of metalwork, painting and palace-building was largely borrowed from an older civilization, the Minoan, on the island of Crete.

The Mycenaean world probably consisted of many rich little kingdoms. Archaeologists have found palaces in several parts of southern Greece, some with enormous royal tombs nearby. To build these must have meant much hard work for ordinary Mycenaeans. It is clear that their rulers had great power over the people.

The Mycenaean civilization was overthrown violently, around 1200 BC. As yet, we do not know who its conquerors were.

Our picture shows the main entrance to Mycenae – the Lion Gate. Laborers struggle to take in a bull for slaughter, while two ladies of the royal family drive out their chariot. Guards on the ramparts wear helmets made with wild boars' tusks.

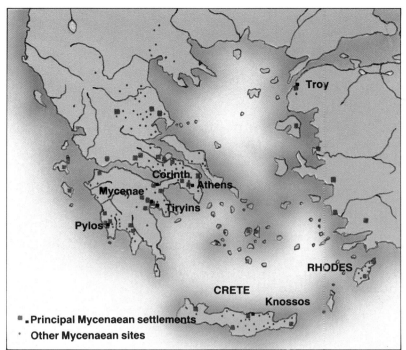

- ■ Principal Mycenaean settlements
- • Other Mycenaean sites

DATECHART

1500s BC The metalwork placed in graves at Mycenae shows that there were fine local craftsmen and rich rulers.

1400s BC Mycenaean Greeks rule the great palace at Knossos on Crete. Mycenaeans had learned much from the Cretans, but now they dominated them.

1400 BC Destruction of Knossos.

1400s-1200s BC The great age of Mycenae. Trade with eastern Mediterranean lands and with Egypt.

1200s BC Huge "beehive tombs" are built at Mycenae, and elsewhere in Greece. The Mycenaean world is threatened. Fortifications are built around its palaces. The Lion Gate is built.

Late 1200s BC The Mycenaeans may have raided the town of Troy in northwest Asia Minor – a raid later remembered as the great Trojan war.

1200 BC The palace at Pylos is captured and burned.

1150 BC Mycenae suffers the same fate. We do not know who the enemy was. It may even have been part of the local population. But more likely the destroyers came from northern Greece. Their fires accidentally baked, and so preserved for us, the many tablets of clay on which palace records were kept.

THE MYCENAEANS

Mycenaean treasure

Greeks down the centuries remembered that Mycenae had been "rich in gold." A German excavator, Heinrich Schliemann, dug at Mycenae in the 19th century (illustrated). He found golden death masks, representing the faces of Mycenae's dead rulers. The most famous is shown on the right. Skilled metalworkers of the period also made ornamental daggers, with different colored metals representing figures in hunting scenes. Copper and gold were imported from abroad.

Hunting boars

Hunting was a favorite pursuit of the Mycenaean aristocracy. Hunting wild boars was exciting and dangerous. Their tusks gave serious wounds, which could easily be fatal. A wall-painting from Tiryns shows that aristocrats of both sexes hunted boars. Afterward, the flesh was eaten and the boar's tusks were sliced lengthwise to form the covering of helmets. Mycenaean figure-of-eight shields were also used in hunting lions.

Tombs

Mycenaean rulers were given high honors even when dead. It was hoped that there was life after death. Several rulers were buried in "beehive tombs." They were magnificent chambers of carefully shaped stone covered with earth. Great wooden platforms were probably used to raise the biggest stones. The lintel over the door of the tomb shown here weighs about 100 tons.

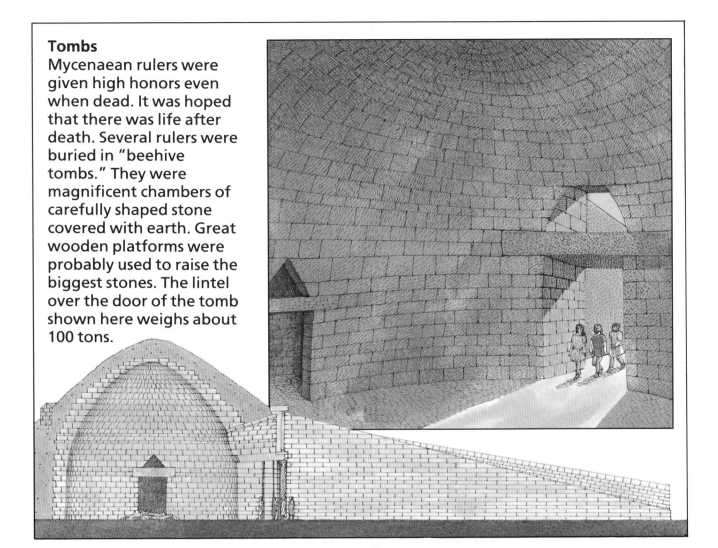

Linear B

Palace scribes wrote on tablets of clay, with signs quite different from the Greek script used in later times. In the 1950s, this early script – "Linear B" – was deciphered and shown to be Greek. The tablets record life just before the Mycenaeans were conquered. They record presents given to the gods – honey and perfumes, for instance. They also show what was in the palace storage rooms, down to broken chariots.

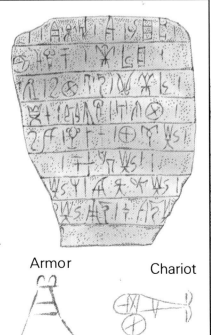

Armor   Chariot

Poems about the Mycenaeans

Two great poems, each as long as a modern novel, have been enjoyed by Greeks through the ages – the *Iliad* and the *Odyssey*. They told of warriors who, led by a king of Mycenae, attacked the fortress city of Troy (shown in the illustration as it was, and in the photograph as it is today). Afterwards the warriors faced terrible dangers returning home.

The storytellers

Greeks thought that the *Iliad* and the *Odyssey* were the work of one poet, Homer. But it is now known that many poets, or "bards," shared in making the poems. They composed orally and learned lines from earlier poets by heart. Bards also added ideas and verses of their own. They recited to music, often to audiences of peaceful country people who loved to hear of adventures and violent deaths.

The Trojan War

The *Iliad* tells of an episode in King Agamemnon's war against the Trojans. The king had been publicly shamed. Queen Helen, wife of his brother, had run away to live with a man in Troy. People had to be reminded of the king's power: Troy had to be beaten.

Characters in the *Iliad* are realistic; they are not just good or bad. Agamemnon himself makes a mistake. He insults his best warrior, Achilles, by taking away his girlfriend. Achilles withdraws, leaving the Trojans free to go on a rampage. The violence is honestly described. Men scream in agony.

Achilles returns when his friend is killed by Prince Hector of Troy. Achilles kills Hector, and drags his corpse around the walls of Troy — watched by Hector's horrified parents.

Odysseus

The hero of the *Odyssey*, Odysseus, is a man of strength and cunning. But he has to fight against the supernatural, and his journey home from Troy takes many years. Some of his men are eaten by a one-eyed monster, the Cyclops. Odysseus escapes by blinding the Cyclops with a wooden stake. Odysseus's boat gets caught in a whirlpool. The hero hangs above the water "like a bat" until the boat reappears.

AGE OF EXPANSION c1000-479 BC

After the fall of the rich Mycenaean towns, Greece entered a period of which little is now known – a dark age. Farmers, fishermen and craftworkers struggled for a living; there was not enough food or land. Many chose, or were forced, to emigrate. They founded colonies on foreign coasts, first in western Asia Minor, then on the Black Sea and the western Mediterranean.

Greek settlements abroad were originally farming communities. But once the settlers were organized, they could trade their extra grain with other cities. This brought some of them great wealth and Greeks in the old homeland joked that some colonists could afford to sleep all day and drink all night!

During this period the Mycenaean form of writing was lost. But after several centuries of illiteracy, Greeks adapted a script from the Phoenicians. Its first letters were alpha and beta; it is the ancestor of our alphabet.

Thera, a small island in the Aegean Sea, sent away some of its people. They sailed to the coast of North Africa and tried to found a colony – without success. Then they returned to Thera. But the people at home were furious. They would not let the men land, but threw things at their boats and forced them to return to Africa. There the colonists succeeded at last in founding the city of Cyrene.

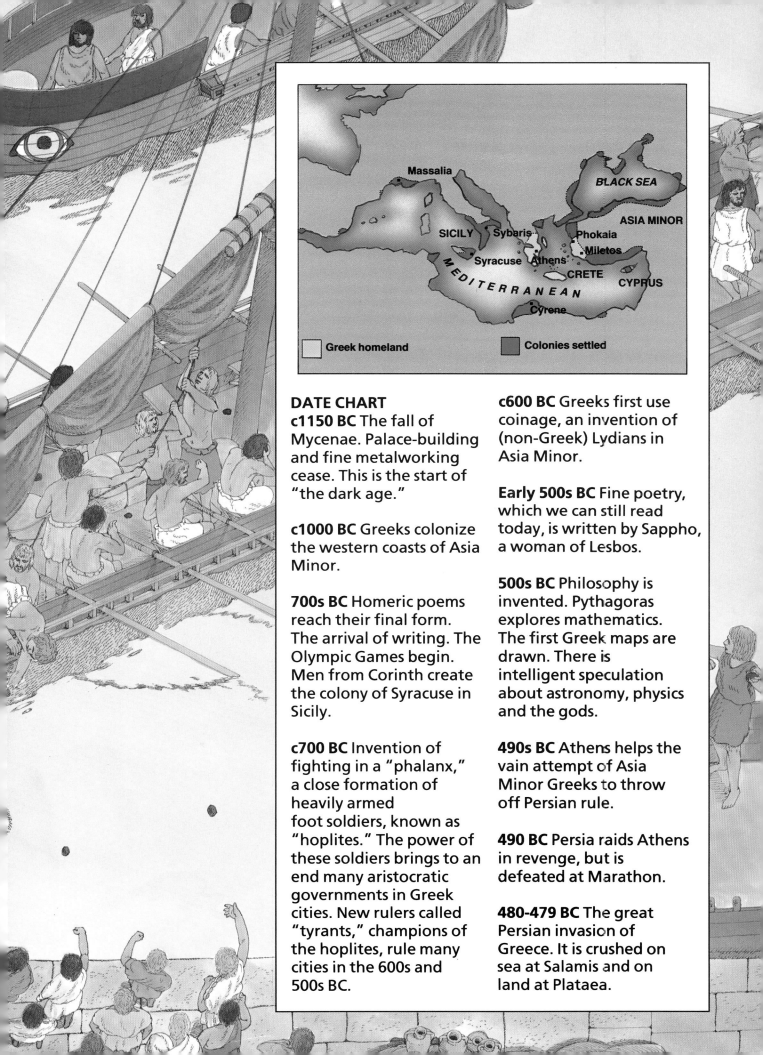

Massalia

BLACK SEA

ASIA MINOR

SICILY — Sybaris — Phokaia
Miletos
Syracuse — Athens
CRETE — CYPRUS
Cyrene

MEDITERRANEAN

Greek homeland

Colonies settled

DATE CHART

c1150 BC The fall of Mycenae. Palace-building and fine metalworking cease. This is the start of "the dark age."

c1000 BC Greeks colonize the western coasts of Asia Minor.

700s BC Homeric poems reach their final form. The arrival of writing. The Olympic Games begin. Men from Corinth create the colony of Syracuse in Sicily.

c700 BC Invention of fighting in a "phalanx," a close formation of heavily armed foot soldiers, known as "hoplites." The power of these soldiers brings to an end many aristocratic governments in Greek cities. New rulers called "tyrants," champions of the hoplites, rule many cities in the 600s and 500s BC.

c600 BC Greeks first use coinage, an invention of (non-Greek) Lydians in Asia Minor.

Early 500s BC Fine poetry, which we can still read today, is written by Sappho, a woman of Lesbos.

500s BC Philosophy is invented. Pythagoras explores mathematics. The first Greek maps are drawn. There is intelligent speculation about astronomy, physics and the gods.

490s BC Athens helps the vain attempt of Asia Minor Greeks to throw off Persian rule.

490 BC Persia raids Athens in revenge, but is defeated at Marathon.

480-479 BC The great Persian invasion of Greece. It is crushed on sea at Salamis and on land at Plataea.

The polis

Ancient Greece, after Mycenaean times, was made up of hundreds of little states. Some were no bigger than villages. Each was known as a *polis*, and had its own government. In some states "oligarchs" ruled – a few rich men who announced their decisions to the people. Others were ruled by a "tyrant," a dictator above the law. From the late 500s BC some Greeks had democracy. Under this system, male citizens held meetings with much laughing and shouting to decide how the polis should be run.

Country life

Most Greeks made their living in the countryside. Here a poor family works on the estate of a wealthy man. His house is in the background, with a tall tower in which his wife and daughters lived a secure and sheltered life. The man plowing uses a plowshare of iron – a metal which came into widespread use after the Mycenaean period. In the background the wife of the plowman collects honey, while his daughter harvests olives with a long stick. His son has hares from a hunt. Much work, indoors and out, was also done by slaves.

One farmer and poet wrote: "Get a woman to follow the plow. But don't marry one – buy one."

The immortals

Most Greeks believed that gods and goddesses controlled events on earth. If lightning struck someone's house, that might be Zeus's anger at work. When a woman died in childbirth, it was the work of Artemis and her "gentle arrows." To attract a boyfriend or girlfriend a person prayed to Aphrodite. Before a sea voyage, a sacrifice of wine was poured to Poseidon, so that he would not cause a shipwreck. Anxious people asked the gods for advice. And to please the gods, temples for them to occupy were built in the loveliest places, on hilltops and headlands with fine views.

1. Artemis (hunting)
2. Asclepius (medicine)
3. Dionysus (wine)
4. Athena (wisdom)
5. Pan (shepherds)
6. Zeus (lord of heaven)
7. Hera (wife of Zeus)
8. Apollo (music and arts)
9. Ares (war)
10. Demeter (corn and earth)
11. Aphrodite (love)
12. Poseidon (sea)

Many farming methods from ancient times are used in Greece today, and women still do much of the work on the land.

Farm produce is often transported by donkeys. The photograph shows a donkey threshing corn in the traditional way.

The life of women

Few women in ancient Greece got an education. Sappho was one. She wrote poems about her girlfriends and about her lovely daughter Cleis.

Women of wealthy families were meant to stay at home. Their main task was to have children — and especially sons — to support the parents later in their old age. A childless woman could be divorced and abandoned. Some women were so afraid of this that they pretended to be pregnant, then smuggled in other women's babies.

Women also prepared raw wool and made clothes from it, as in the picture below. (The photograph shows a Greek woman today weaving in the traditional way.) To have a suntan suggested that a woman worked outdoors because she was poor. So rich, fashionable women were proud to be pale.

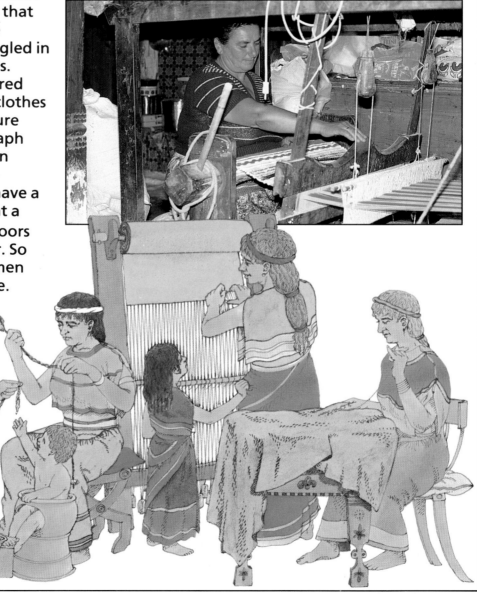

The Persian Wars
Stretching away to the east of Greece was the vast Persian Empire. It included most of the Middle East, and had far greater resources than Greece. In 490 BC King Darius of Persia sent a fairly small force to attack Athens, which the Athenians defeated at Marathon. According to legend a messenger ran with news of victory to Athens – the original Marathon run!

Persia had to gain revenge, otherwise her subjects might think her weak and revolt. So in 480 BC Persia sent an enormous invasion force, hundreds of thousands of men by land and sea, under King Xerxes. The Greeks were terrified, but did not panic. Three hundred Spartan hoplites went bravely to their deaths, trying to block the pass of Thermopylae against the Persians.

At the battle of Salamis (illustrated) the Persian fleet was tricked into fighting in a narrow space. The slower, heavier, Greek ships crashed triumphantly into the crowded enemy. Xerxes fled. The full Greek land army, led by Sparta, crushed his remaining troops on land at Plataea.

THE GOLDEN AGE 478-405 BC

After Salamis, Athens' ships dominated the Aegean Sea. Other Greek states allied with Athens, and paid her to organize naval raids on Persian territory. By degrees this alliance became an Athenian empire. Athenian warships protected traders and captured pirates. They forced other Greeks to adopt democracy, as Athens had, and made them pay tax to Athens.

With this new income, Athens entered a "golden age." Superb temples were built which still stand today. The most important was the Parthenon. There was also wealth to produce drama, and new and shocking ideas were expressed about society and the gods. But Athens' rise was watched with dread by her rivals – the Spartans. Cunning, brave and savage, the Spartans crushed Athens after long years of war.

A scene from the 440s BC. On the acropolis ("high city") of Athens, the Parthenon, Athena's great temple, is being built. Some Greeks called it Athens' "pretty face." Behind wooden scaffolding, columns rise, made of stone drums. Citizens admire the sculpture to be placed above the columns.

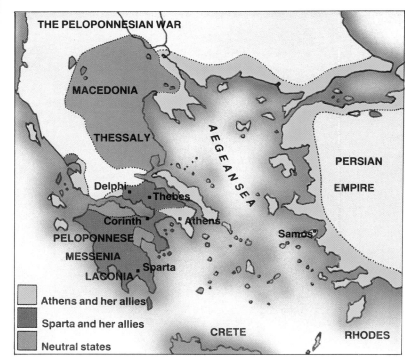

THE PELOPONNESIAN WAR

MACEDONIA

THESSALY

A E G E A N S E A

PERSIAN
EMPIRE

Delphi
Thebes
Corinth
Athens
PELOPONNESE
Samos
MESSENIA
Sparta
LACONIA

Athens and her allies

Sparta and her allies

Neutral states

CRETE
RHODES

DATECHART

477 BC Athens leads a new alliance against Persia.

469 BC Her admiral Cimon crushes the Persian fleet in the eastern Mediterranean.

c460-455 BC An Athenian fleet tries to dominate Egypt. However, it is stranded and captured when the Persians cunningly drain the water from under it.

c460-446 BC The first Peloponnesian War – Sparta and her allies against Athens and hers – ends in a draw.

Mid and late 400s BC Age of great Athenian dramatists. Athens encourages – or forces – many allies to adopt democracy.

447 BC Athens begins building the Parthenon. Soon after comes the complex gateway building, the *Propylaea*. This is even more impressive to Greeks.

431 BC Sparta, seeing an Athenian weakness, begins the great Peloponnesian War.

421 BC The first stage of the war ends, with Athens slightly ahead.

415 BC Athens invades Sicily, and seeks to become queen of the Mediterranean.

413 BC Athens loses her great invasion force at Syracuse in Sicily.

404 BC Sparta and allies starve Athens into surrender.

THE GOLDEN AGE

Life in Athens

The Athenian democracy was famous for free speech. Ordinary men were not afraid of the authorities, because in many ways they *were* the authorities. Rich men complained that the poor and even the donkeys wouldn't get out of their way in the street!

Athens was an open city. Foreigners brought new ideas. There were many festivals, with free food. Money was given to the poor to buy theater tickets. Actors wore masks, but still they made the audience feel terror and sympathy during a tragedy. Comedy was more relaxed. The audience was merry from drinking. The actors made rude jokes and criticized politicians.

Greek ideas

Athens became the center of Greek ideas. Athenians practiced philosophy – a Greek invention. Wise men like Socrates asked intelligent questions, which revealed that ordinary ideas about knowledge and justice were too shallow. At drinking parties men would learn by discussing and criticizing each others' ideas.

Life in Sparta

At Sparta there was less fun and freedom than at Athens. The city was like an army camp. Spartans feared that their unfree workers, the *helots*, would attack. So they trained to become good soldiers. Cowards were hit and insulted. This was to teach Spartans to face death bravely on the battlefield. They called themselves "the similars." Anyone who was a bit different was unpopular. Books and new ideas were not welcome.

Boys were taught to steal and lie, to make them cunning warriors. The cheese-stealing contest, shown here, taught them to be brave but also how to avoid being hit.

Schools and education

Athenian boys went to school, but girls did not. Girls were meant to learn from their mothers at home. The boys were taught to read and write and also to respect the wisdom in the old poems of Homer.

Probably the teaching of boys was rather relaxed, without written examinations. This may be one reason why Greeks in adult life still found learning to be fun. Greek men were said to be like children, because they kept on asking intelligent questions.

THE GOLDEN AGE

Decisions at Athens

Big decisions, such as whether to go to war, were made by mass meetings of Athenian male citizens. These ordinary men had much more power than in most countries today.

Election was used to choose generals, such as the aristocrat Pericles (far right). But most official jobs were awarded by lot, so that ordinary people would get them. A man who was too powerful could be "ostracized" – sent away for 10 years. Voters, like those shown here, wrote his name on *ostraka*, bits of broken pot.

Hoplite

- Helmet
- Cuirass
- Sword
- Spear
- Shield
- Greaves

Land warfare

The main force in most land battles was the phalanx, formed of heavily armed hoplites in lines. They had large shields, and fought shoulder to shoulder, moving slowly. Archers could damage them and so cavalry was used to chase these opponents away. A hoplite killed by thrusting a spear at an enemy's neck. Below, a hoplite arms while his wife and father look on.

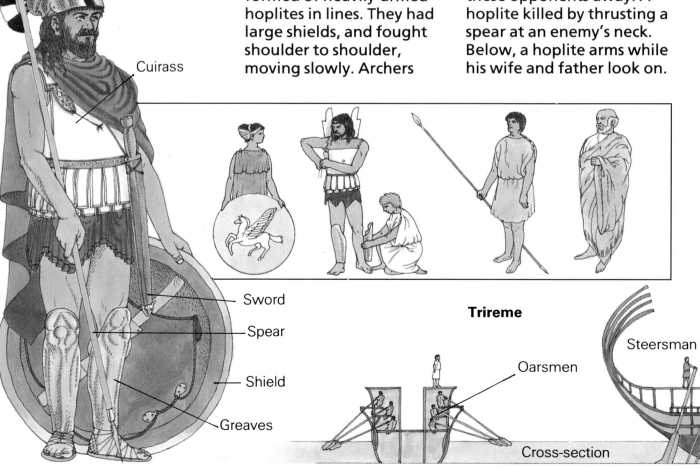

Trireme

- Steersman
- Oarsmen
- Cross-section

The Peloponnesian War

Spartans dreaded that Athens would one day dominate the area of southern Greece which Sparta controlled, the Peloponnese. So Sparta's policy was to wait for a moment of Athenian weakness, then to attack.

In 431 BC Spartans and their allies burned the farms and homes around Athens (shown here), challenging the Athenians to come out and fight. Advised by Pericles, the Athenians sensibly refused to fight. Instead, Athens' city walls kept the Spartans out, while her fleet brought in food and money. After 413 BC, Sparta built a fleet of her own and cut off Athens' corn supply. Hunger forced Athens to surrender in 404 BC and Sparta took over her empire.

Sea warfare

For a long time Athens dominated at sea. Her fleet at one point had 300 "triremes," ships in which the rowers were arranged on three levels. Each trireme had a crew of about 200. A pipe-player helped the rowers to move their oars in time.

A trireme's crew aimed to maneuver until the ram at the front of their ship could crash into the weakest part of an enemy ship – its side section. The enemy ship would then break and sink. Its sailors drowned or were speared in the water.

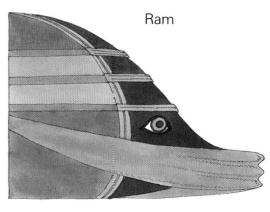

Ram

Marines

Archers

THE HELLENISTIC AGE 336-30 BC

After the fall of Athens, Greece was dominated first by Sparta, then by Thebes. But both were poor cities, and growing in strength on the northern border of Greece was an enemy who owned a gold mine – Philip of Macedon.

Philip's gold bought him allies in Greece, and a professional army, fighting winter and summer. Philip and his experienced men proved too much for the Greek hoplites, most of whom fought seldom and spent winter on their farms. By 338 BC the Macedonians had control of Greece.

In 336 BC Philip was murdered. His son and heir, Alexander, was 20 and less than 5ft tall. "Just a boy," sneered his enemies. But the boy did what Greek men had often dreamed of: he conquered the Persian empire. Alexander and later rulers spread Greek – Hellenic – language and customs from Egypt to northwest India.

For long the Persian empire had been protected by its sheer size. But Alexander's troops were unusually obedient, and marched vast distances at his command. He won his men's respect partly by his courage. The picture shows the battle of Issus in Syria, where Alexander (left) met the inexperienced King Darius III of Persia (right).

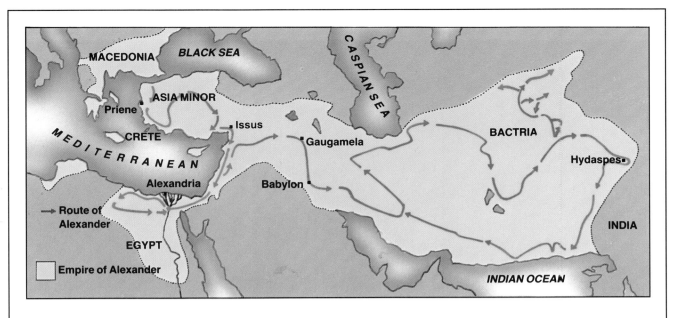

DATECHART

336 BC Alexander inherits Macedonia and Greece.

334 BC Alexander invades the Persian empire and wins Asia Minor.

333-1 BC Alexander crushes King Darius III at Issus and at Gaugamela

and takes over the Persian Empire. He founds Alexandria in Egypt.

326 BC Alexander's conquests in Punjab, northwest India.

323 BC Alexander dies at Babylon. His generals

divide his empire. Seleucos and his descendants got Asia; Ptolemy and his family got Egypt and Alexandria.

40s-30s BC The last Ptolemy, Clecpatra VII, loses her kingdom to Rome.

THE HELLENISTIC AGE

Alexandria, city of learning
Alexander founded many cities called Alexandria. The greatest was on the northern coast of Egypt. It became the leading center of learning. Scholars from abroad received generous salaries at the *Mouseion* (the original Museum).

The great lighthouse of Alexandria, the Pharos (right), was used by the merchants who sailed to India and the east.

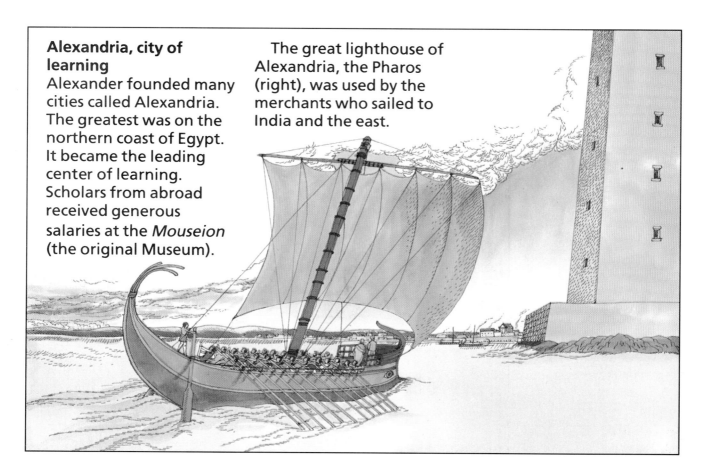

The new learning
Hellenistic rulers had great power over their subjects, and were often worshipped as gods. Writers who criticized or offended them were punished. So the Hellenistic world produced romantic poetry and science. These subjects were relatively safe!

The science of medicine flourished at Alexandria. Herophilos was the first to study anatomy by cutting up human bodies. Much was learned about the parts of the body, and also about the causes of illnesses and deaths. Another doctor, Erasistratos, made important discoveries about the circulation of the blood.

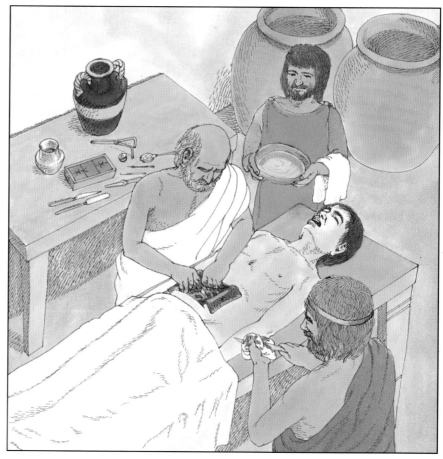

Mathematics

The scientists of Alexandria worked out the size of the earth using geometry. Eratosthenes saw that in southern Egypt a vertical sundial cast no shadow at the summer solstice; the sun was directly overhead. But at the same moment, sundials *did* cast shadow in Alexandria, in the north of Egypt. By measuring the angle of that shadow, and the distance between the northern and southern sundials, he worked out with 90% accuracy the circumference of the earth.

Inventions

Many things were invented at this time. Archimedes invented machines of war.

These included a crane to grab and upset enemy ships. It was also said he invented a device using mirrors to burn ships. Heron of Alexandria built a steam engine.

Industrial production was despised as slaves' work. The picture shows Archimedes at a forge. Blacksmiths are fitting iron bands to a device now known as Archimedes' screw. This is a machine for raising water from one level to another. The photograph above shows the screw still in use in Egypt.

Alexander in the east

Alexander was not content with conquering the Persian Empire. He tried to reach the end of the world. This was thought to be the east coast of India. In the way stood the army of an Indian king, Porus, with terrifying war elephants. Alexander won the battle of Hydaspes and marched on into India (326 BC). But at last his tired soldiers said "No more." They were afraid they would never get home. Alexander pretended to sulk, saying that he would go on alone. But the troops stood firm. At last it was announced, to a great cheer, that they could turn back. The soldiers had done what the enemies could not: they had stopped Alexander.

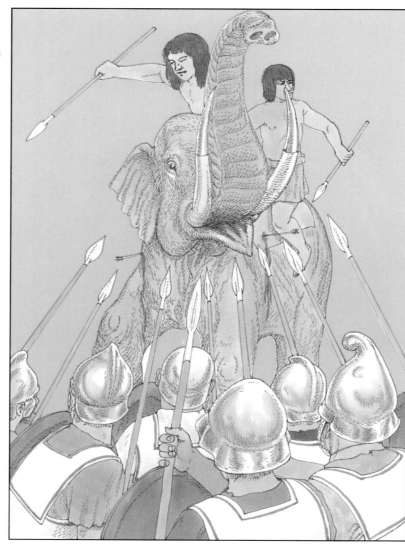

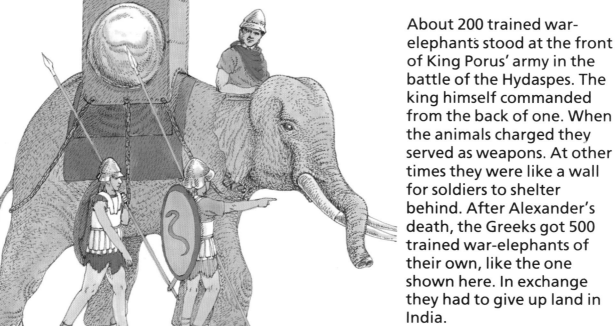

About 200 trained war-elephants stood at the front of King Porus' army in the battle of the Hydaspes. The king himself commanded from the back of one. When the animals charged they served as weapons. At other times they were like a wall for soldiers to shelter behind. After Alexander's death, the Greeks got 500 trained war-elephants of their own, like the one shown here. In exchange they had to give up land in India.

The range of the empire

Alexander's empire was enormous. The coins shown below were from just three of its many parts: Crete, Egypt and Persia. They all carry Alexander's head.

To guard the far-away east of his empire, Alexander left soldiers to colonize Bactria and north-west India. When Alexander died, they tried to march west again. But they were forced back with the help of Persian cavalry. Alexander's generosity to the Persians worked: they were now defending their dead conqueror's empire. Some Greeks in India and Bactria formed lively independent kingdoms. We show the remains at Priene, a Hellenistic city in Asia Minor.

Greek influence on Rome

The Romans eventually conquered the main Hellenistic kingdoms. But Greek ideas lived on. Most Roman writers modeled their work on Greek literature. Greek slaves and ex-slaves acquired great power. The picture shows one of them advising a Roman emperor. In the early AD 300s the capital of the Roman empire was moved from Rome to a Greek city – Constantinople. The people of the new capital were proud to call themselves "the Romans" – in Greek!

Many of the ideas of Ancient Greece were so intelligent or entertaining that they have attracted people from many times. During the Middle Ages, the long centuries in which Christianity dominated Europe, most Greek literature was lost forever. But from the fifteenth century people rediscovered how interesting the Greeks had been.

From that time until the present day, some schools have taught ancient Greek. Greek writings on politics and religion are still read with respect by many people. And modern scientists, when they want new words for new notions, often make them up — like "catalyst" and "electron" — from the language of the Greeks.

The Olympic Games

Today's Olympic Games are not very old. They began in 1896. They are modeled on the ancient Greek games, which were held every four years at Olympia. Like the modern Olympics (right), the ancient games were the supreme contest for athletes. Ancient Greek states, like nations today, used athletes for propaganda. They fixed races and bribed umpires!

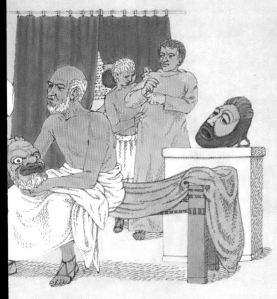

The theater
Drama seems to have originally grown from a simple chorus, which sang in honor of the god Dionysus. The illustration shows a famous playwright of Ancient Greece – Aeschylus – with his players. Plays were presented in theaters specially built into a hillside so that as many people as possible could see. Some of these theaters are still used today (above), and their design has been copied in many modern theaters.

Doric   Ionic   Corinthian

Architecture
Greek architecture is famous for its tall columns. They decorated important buildings, such as the Parthenon (above) in ancient times. Today, many towns have buildings in the Greek style, especially buildings where people go to think, like libraries and museums.

INDEX

Photographic Credits:
Pages 8 and 31 (top): C. M. Dixon/ Photoresources; page 10: Ronald Sheridan/ Ancient Art and Architecture; pages 15 and 16: Robert Harding; page 29: Spectrum; page 30: Leo Mason; page 31 (bottom): Greg Evans.